COMICS MAGAZINE

SPECIAL EDITION
OCT/2017

BLANK COMIC
BOOK

- Laluna Comics -

THE BEST STORIES
EVERY MONTH

STOP!!!

First of all, test your colors...

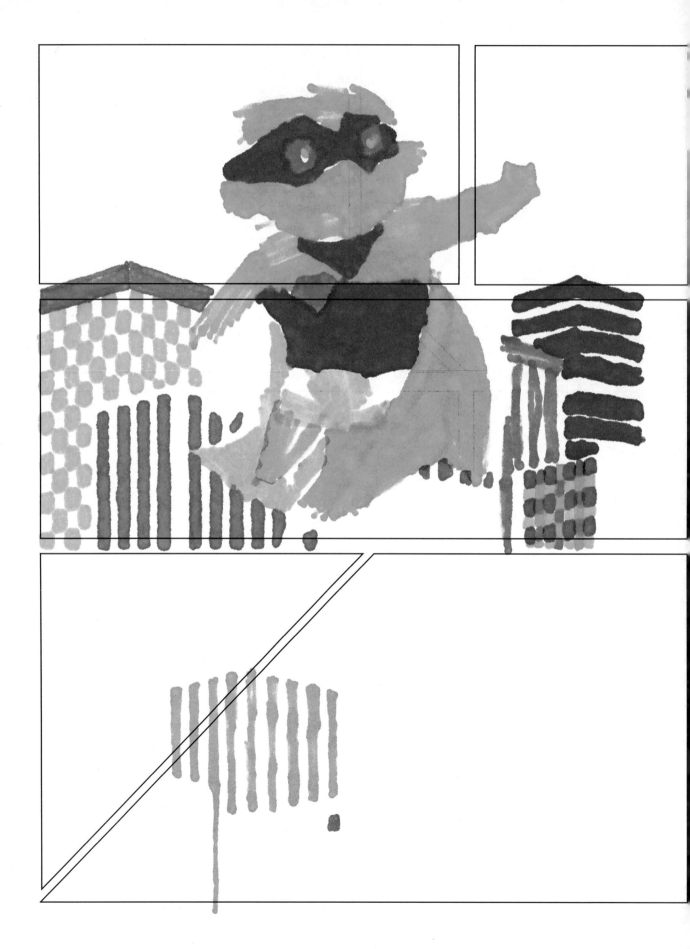

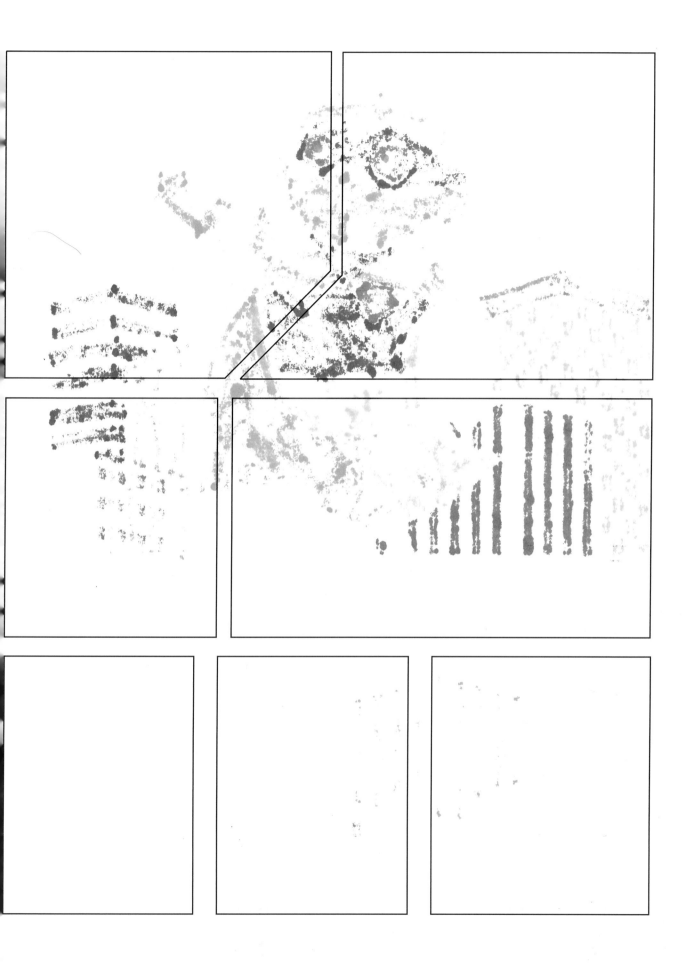

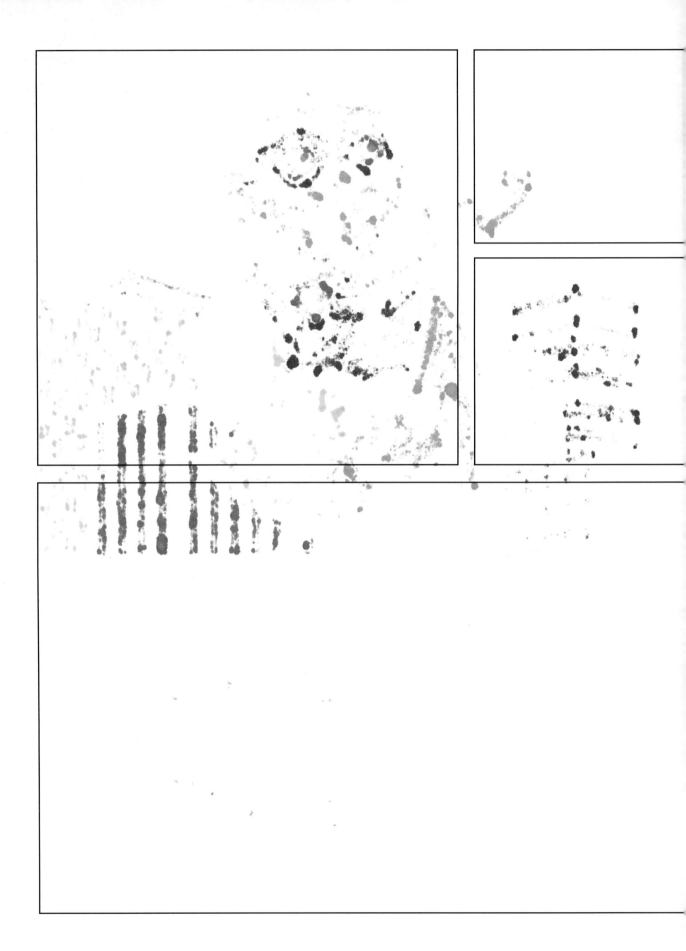

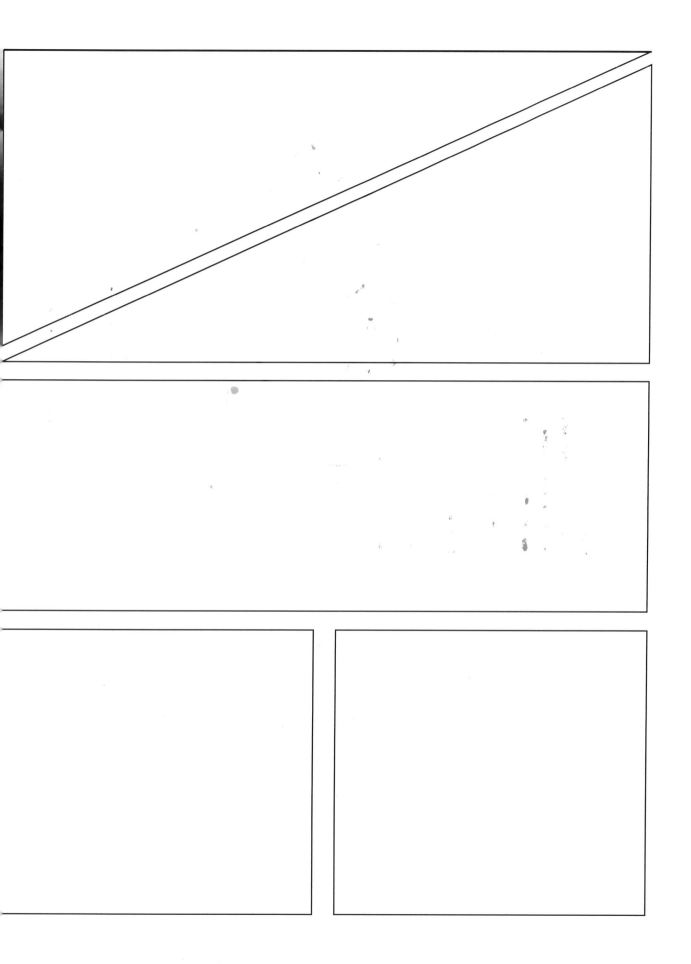

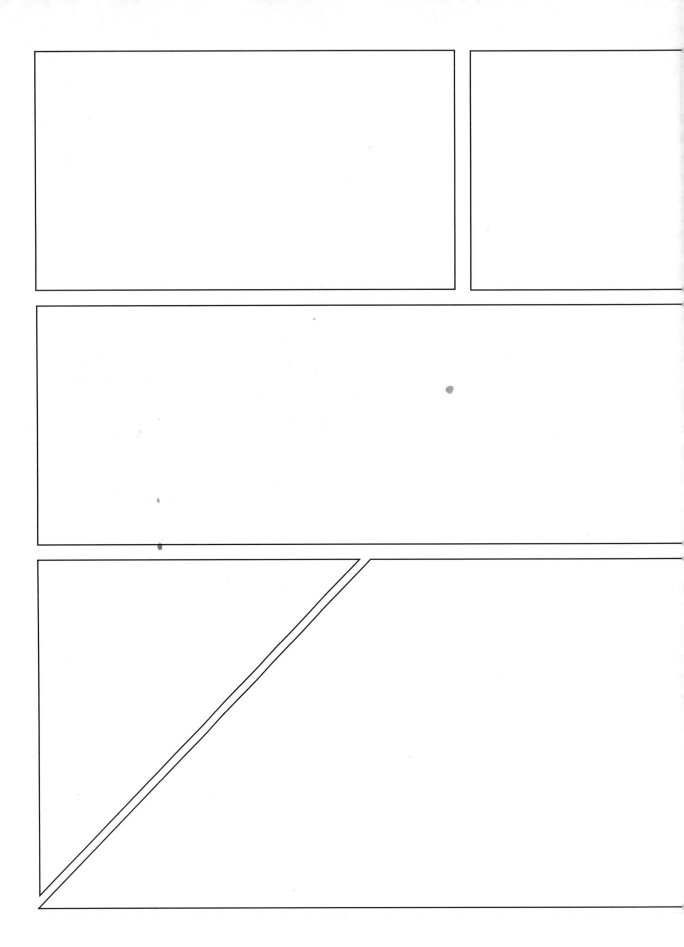

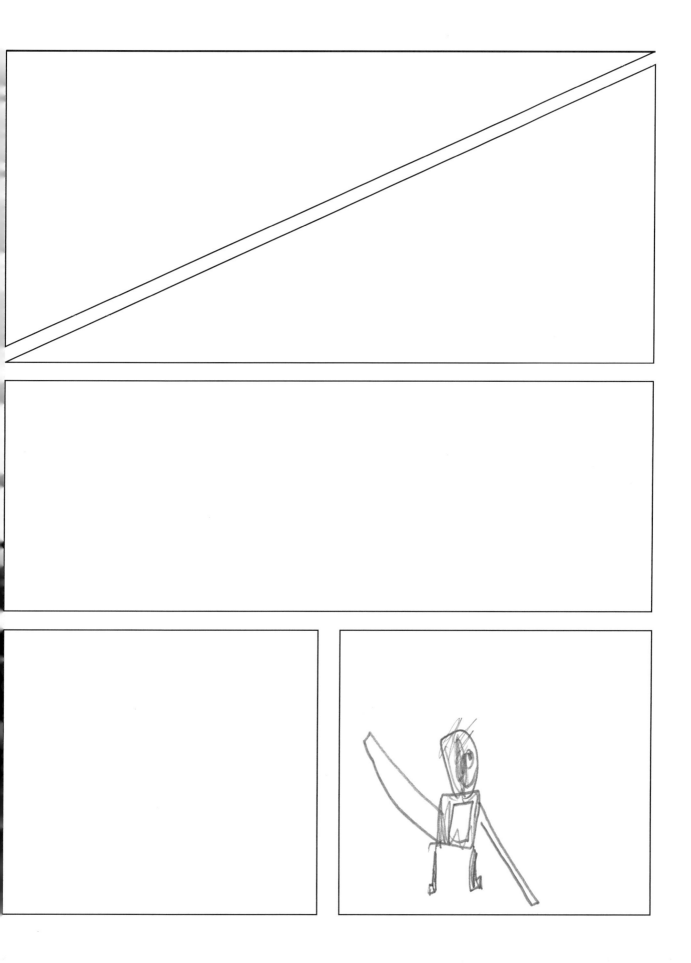

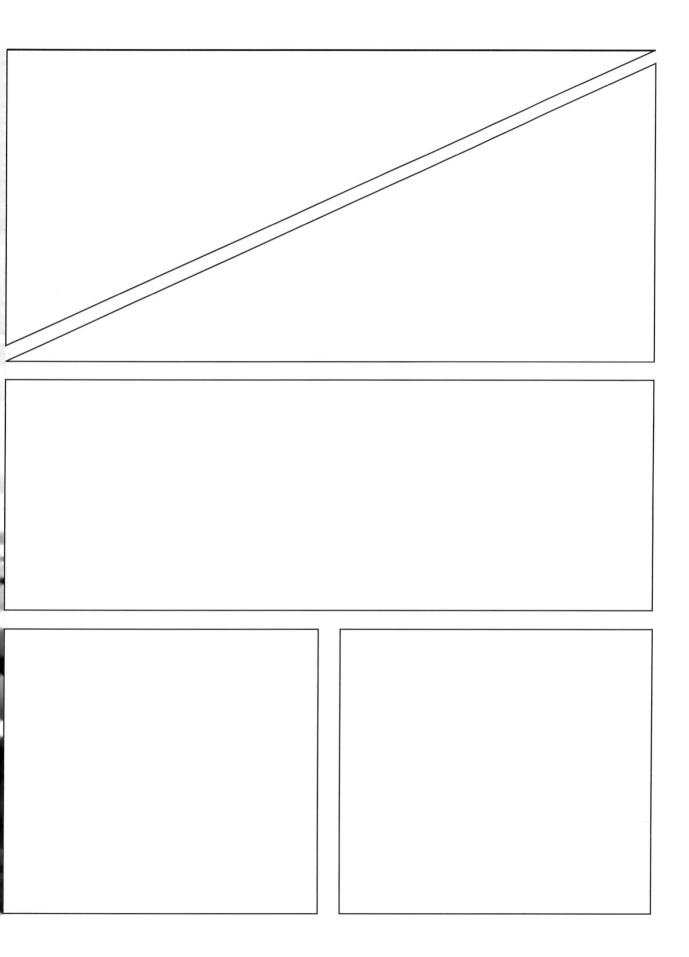

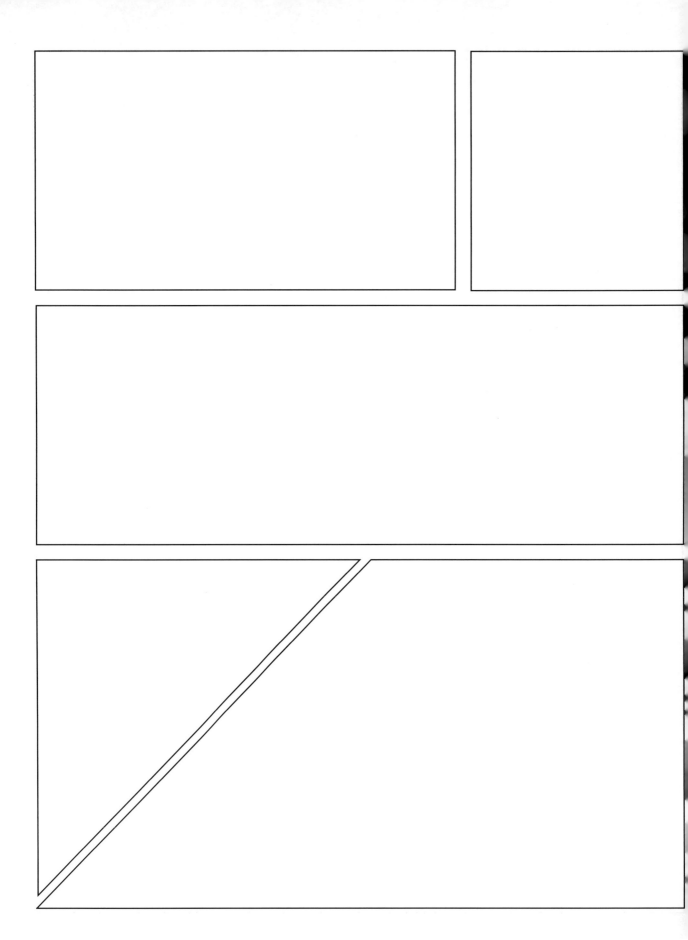

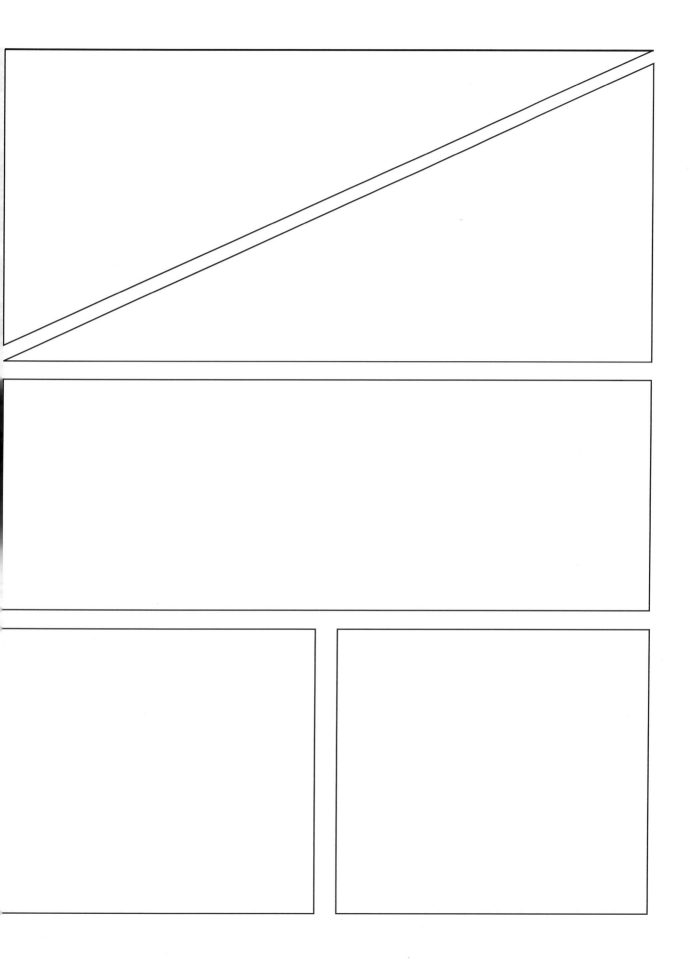

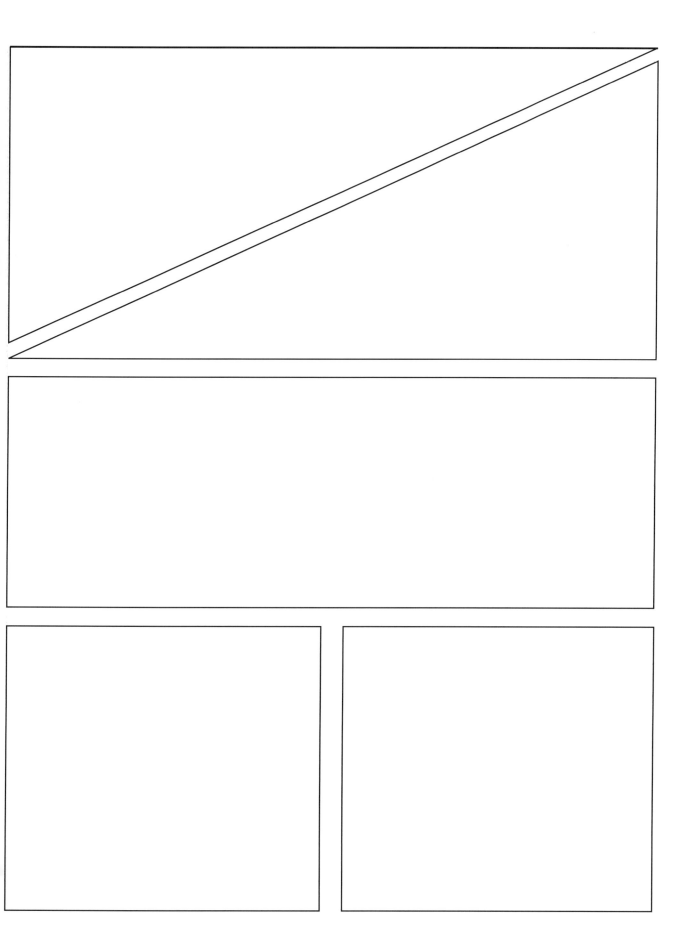

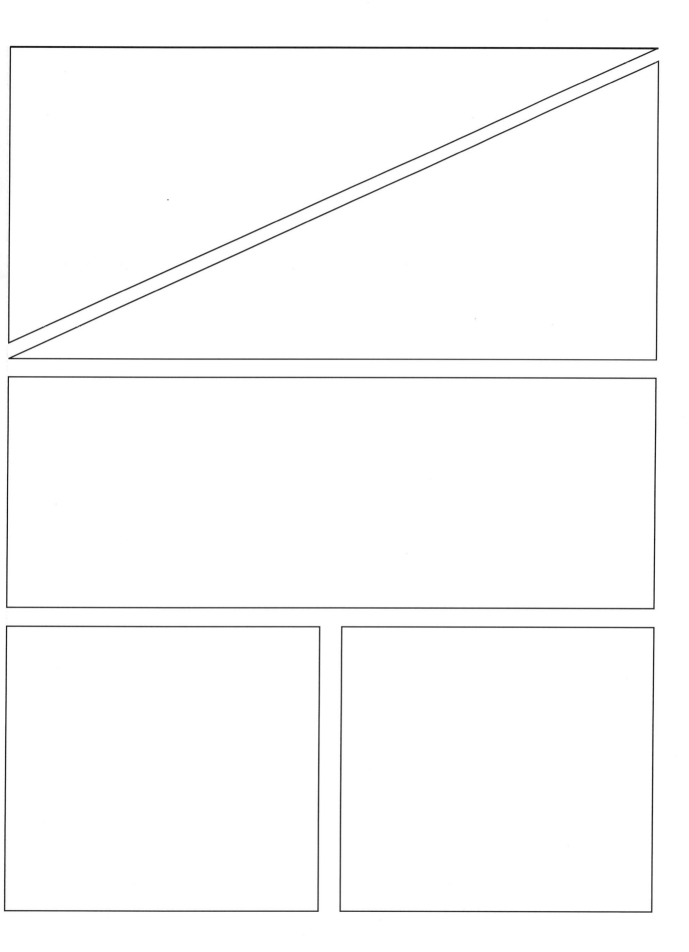

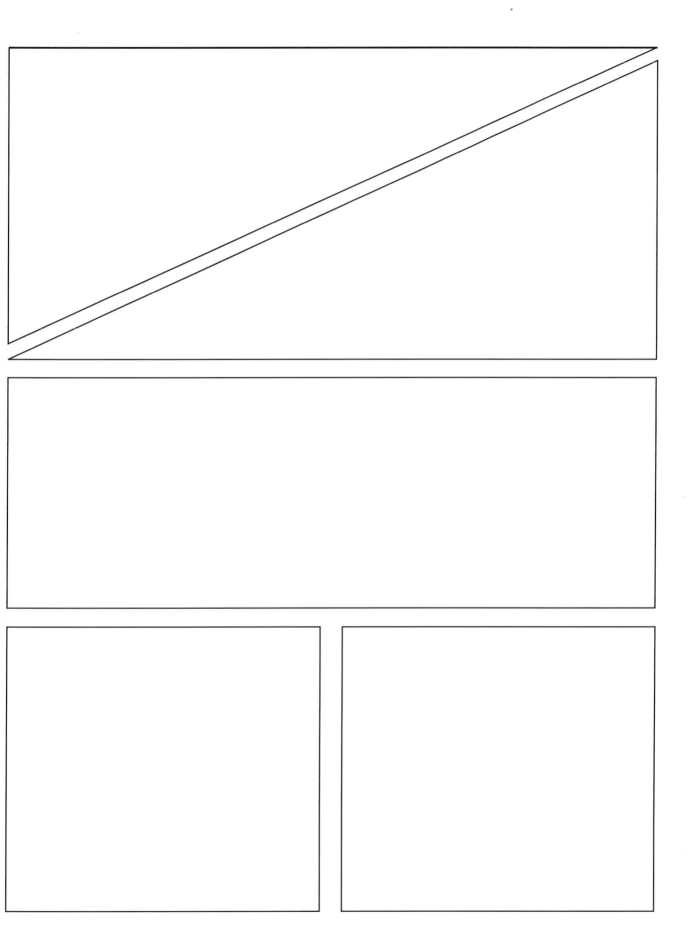

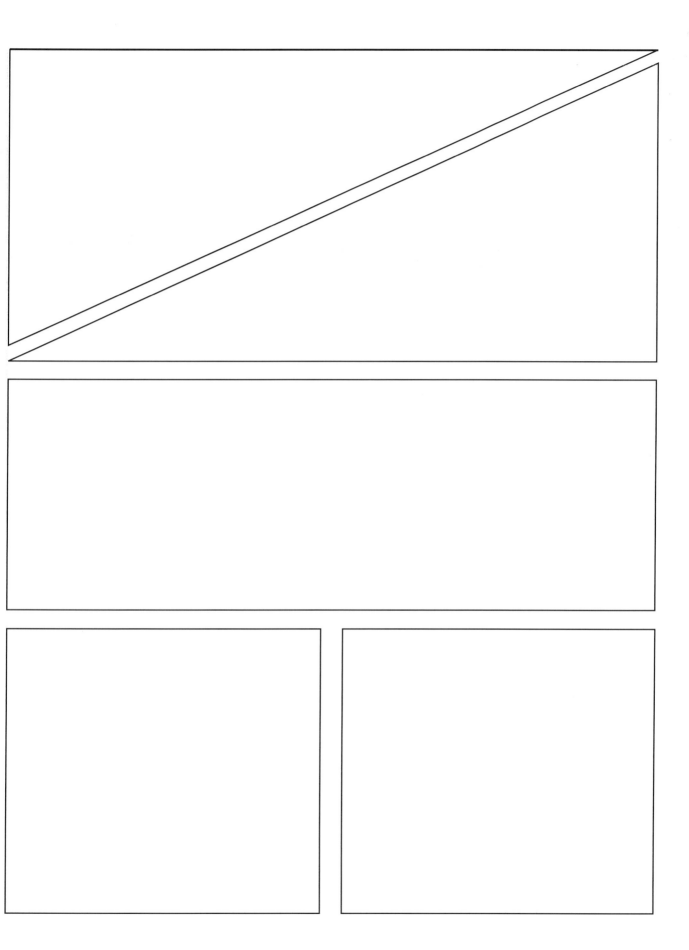

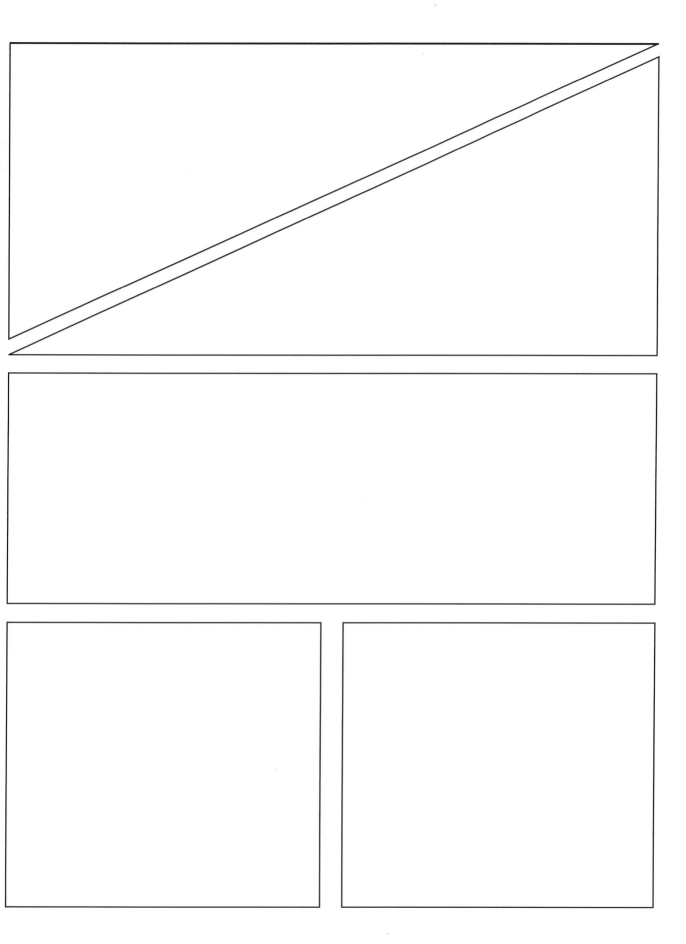

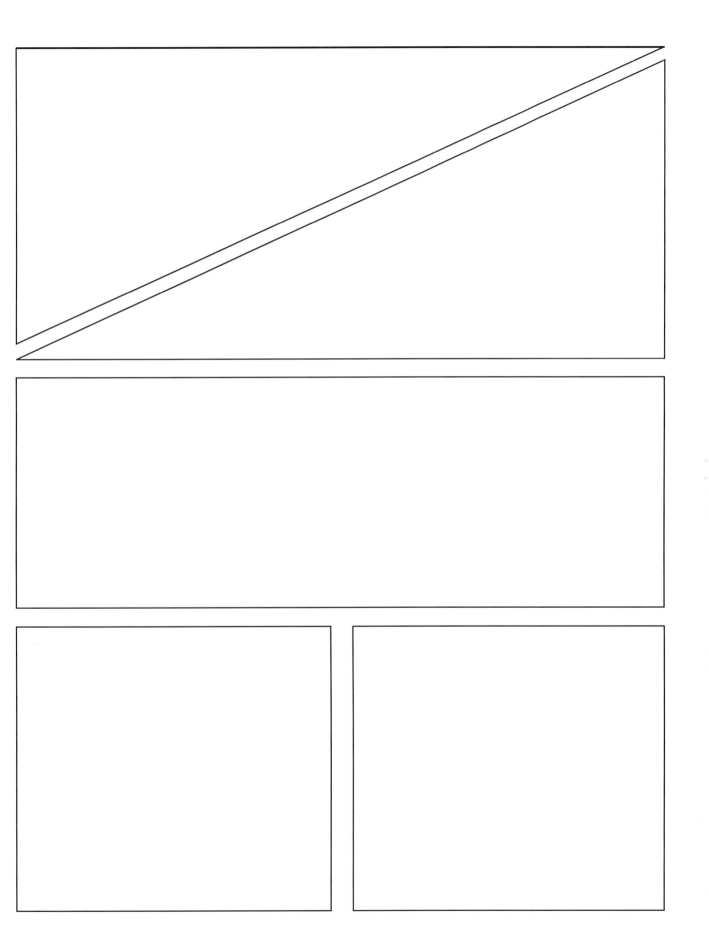

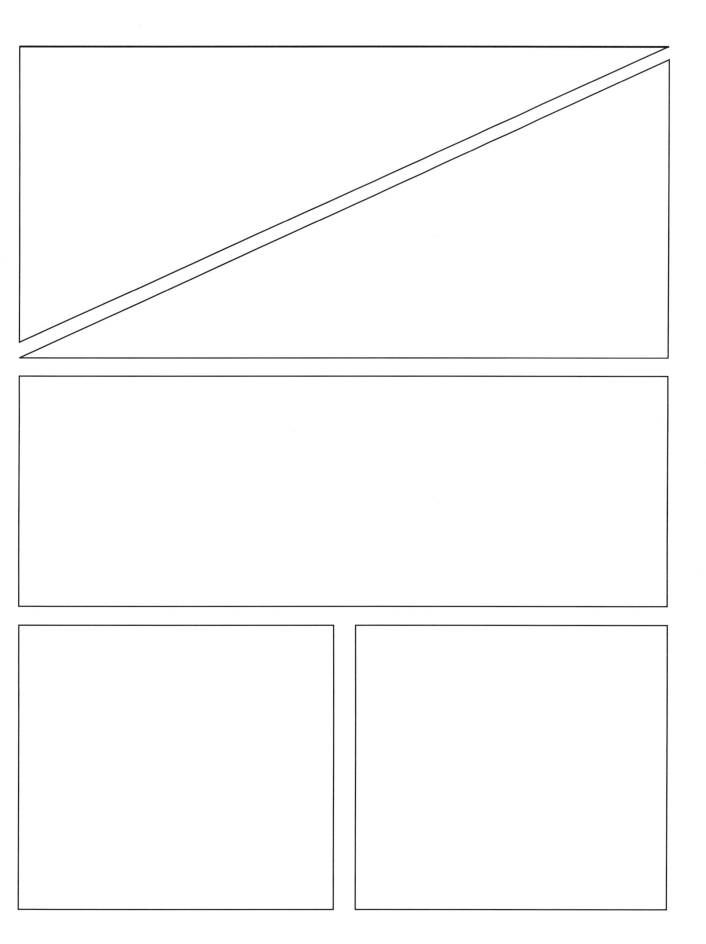

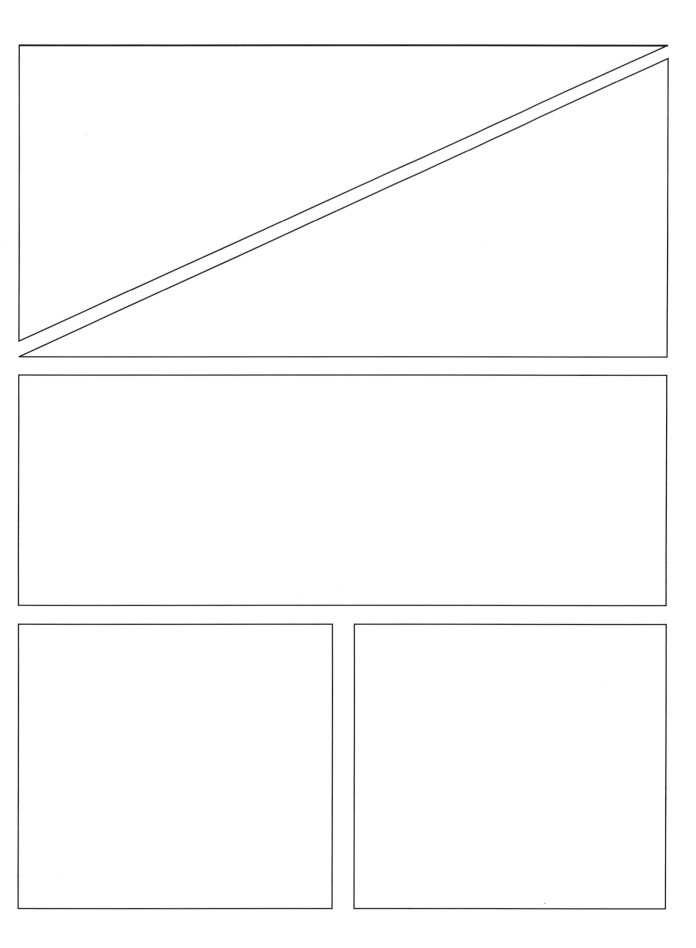

121

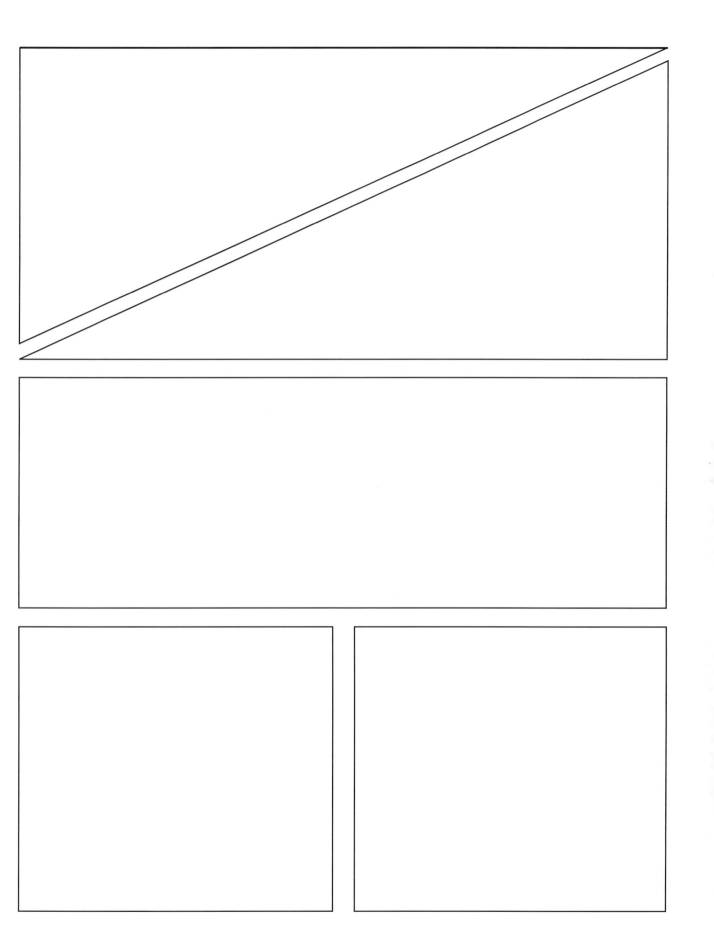

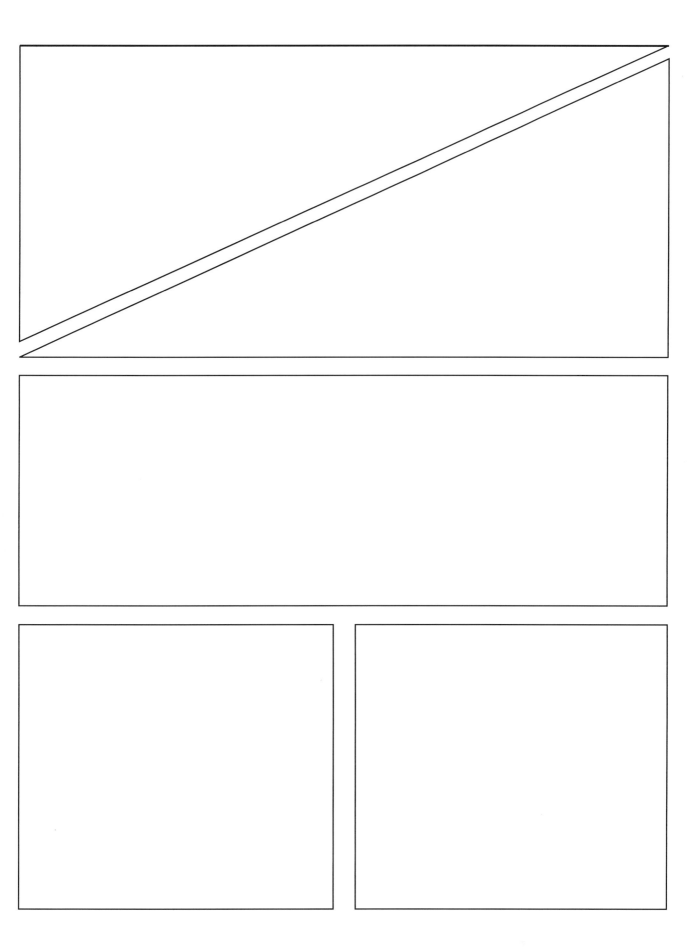

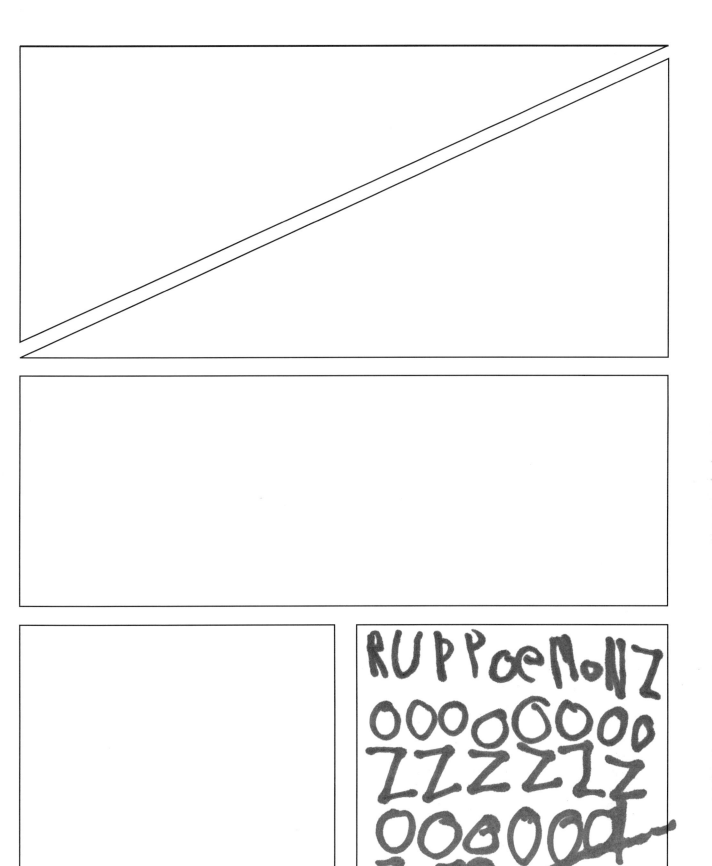

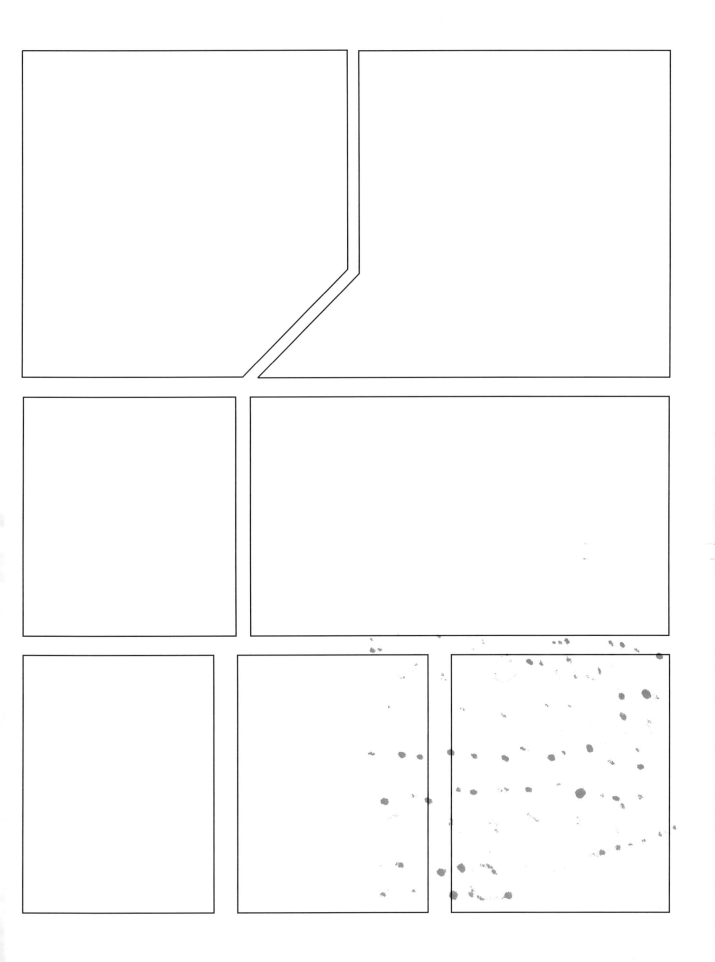

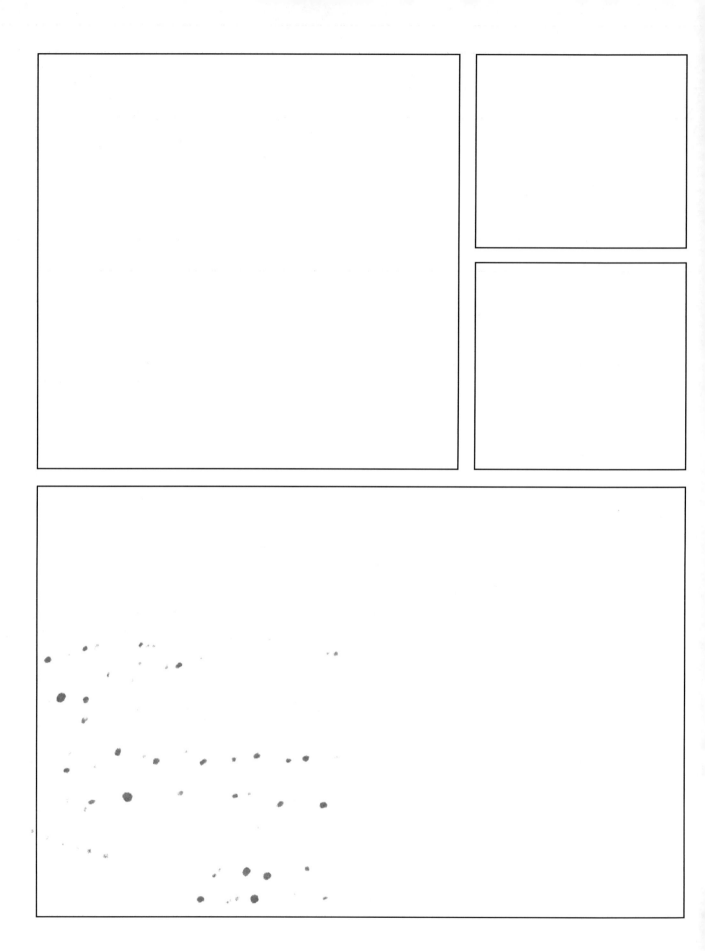

Made in the USA
Columbia, SC
25 November 2018